THE COMING

THREE DAYS OF DARKNESS

The Coming
Three Days of Darkness

JOANNE M. BALLINGER

Ballinger Dev. LLC | Rancho Mirage

Copyright © 2015

Ballinger Dev. LLC, Rancho Mirage, California

First Printing, 2015

Printed in the United States of America

ISBN   978-0-692-60605-6

Table of Contents

Foreword

What is the prophecy of the three days of darkness? Sacred Scripture, saints, and prophets, have foretold days of darkness to encompass the earth towards the end of times. What is the significance and meaning of this prophecy and are there current signs of the approaching darkness? Are there ways to prepare for this dark prophecy?

As a Catholic, I have always heard of the impending three days of darkness. I recollect being told to always place a blessed cross above all the doors of the house and always have a blessed "beeswax" candle available. But, I had limited knowledge of this prophecy.

Growing up in the 70's and 80's, I was also told there would come a time when people would not know what sin is. Impossible to believe at the time, I see now, in 2015, that this time has come. The secular progressive view and the majority of the new generation believe sin is an indiscretion with no accountability.

Numerous saints and visionaries, living in different areas of the world, and at different time periods, have predicted the coming three days of darkness. Many passages in the Bible also appear to allude to the three days of darkness. As we read in the Bible, God's revelation to the prophets were handed down through the generations. The watchful looked for the signs as described, and knew that the prophecy would be fulfilled. We see this when the three Kings observed the star as foretold and knew the Messiah had been born.

Prophecies from Holy ones should be taken seriously. Events were used to describe when a revelation would be fulfilled, not specific dates. We should be cautious if a prophecy contains a specific date or time.

In this book, we'll discuss the prophecy of the three days of darkness. Why does the present time precipitate a divine justice? Why would these days of darkness be inevitable? Current events indicate this prophecy is closer than ever before! What can you do to prepare, and more importantly, what not to do. This prophecy applies to all of us. Catholic, or not, this book might just save your life!

To Saint Anne, Mother of the Blessed Virgin Mary

Dedicated to my loving mother

"Be on your guard, stand firm in the faith, be courageous, be strong." St. Paul

I

Prophecy by the Saints and Mystics

Throughout history people believed they were living in end times. The present time is no different. However, we know from the Bible, the Lord, since the beginning of time has utilized the Patriarchs and holy people to prophecy coming events just as they prophesied His first coming. Then, and now, there are skeptics who question whether Jesus was in fact God's son or just a holy prophet. They were not ready to believe the prophecies were fulfilled. Why should we not heed the warnings given by a numerous amount of saints and prophets?

Many of these prophecies included "signs" of the impending prophecy. Vigilant people were aware when these signs were present and prepared. There will be many who question the prophecy of the three days of darkness. Do you feel an impending disaster awaits us? Do you feel God's justice is inevitable for the atrocities committed against Christians daily? Saints and mystics recognized by the Church for their holiness have predicted the coming three days of darkness to envelope the entire earth. These saints give detailed information on what is forthcoming and how to act and pray during this purification.

Before delving into the prophecies of the saints, let's examine the definition of a saint and why their predictions would be worth considering. A saint is a person who has been canonized by the Catholic Church as one who has lived a holy and exemplary life. They possessed virtues of charity and heroic virtue.

In the early days of the Church martyrs were publicly venerated by the people, but to be lawful the local Bishop, after investigation, must approve it. This was the first known process of Beatification. Later in the Church the beatification and canonization process was permitted only by the Holy See (the Pope). This process involves rigid scrutiny by the Church and exhaustive investigation into the life of the deceased individual.

The Church process of canonization includes three stages: Venerable, Blessed, and Sainthood. During the investigation process, miracle(s) attributed by the intercession of the deceased must also be found to be valid. The number of miracles depends on the investigation process. These miracles are also seriously scrutinized during the investigation, and are not easily accepted until several conditions are met.

One can be confident that a deceased person's life was intensively investigated, and that the declared "Saint" deserves our respect and honor. Therefore, we can feel confident that the writings and predictions of the saints were not merely written without conviction. The predictions set forth were made by individuals who have been declared by the Catholic Church as either Venerable, Blessed, or Saints.

Blessed Anna Maria Taigi was one of the many saints who predicted the coming three days of darkness. She was born in Siena, Italy on May 29, 1769, and died in 1837. She was beatified by Pope Benedict XV on May 20, 1920. Blessed Anna Maria Taigi is one of the incorruptible saints whose body remains preserved. She was successful in predicting World War I and II. She was an ideal mother and housewife who was a model of Christian life. Blessed Taigi's extraordinary gifts are described in the book "Wife, Mother and Mystic" written by Albert Bessieres S.J. She had the ability to read souls and know what illnesses they suffered and how to cure them. Influential people came to her for advice. She performed miracles curing the sick. She prayed for the souls in purgatory and they were known to visit her after their release from purgatory and thank her. Blessed Taigi could clearly see the past, present, and future.

Blessed Anna Maria Taigi predicts:

God will send two punishments; one will be in the form of wars, revolutions and other evils; it shall originate on earth. The other will be sent from heaven. There shall come over the whole earth an intense darkness lasting three days and three nights. Nothing can be seen, and the air will be laden with pestilence which will claim many, but not only, the enemies of religion. It will be impossible to use any man-made lighting during this darkness, except blessed candles. He, who out of curiosity, opens his window to look out, or leaves his home, will fall dead on the spot. During these three days, people should remain in their homes, pray the Rosary and beg God for mercy.

All the enemies of the Church, whether known or unknown, will perish over the whole earth during that universal darkness, with the exception of a few whom God will soon convert. The air shall be infected by demons who will appear under all sorts of hideous forms. Religion shall be persecuted, and priests massacred, Churches shall be closed, but only for a short time. The Holy Father shall be obliged to leave Rome.

France shall fall into a frightful anarchy. The French shall have a desperate civil war in the course of which even old men will take up arms. The political parties, having exhausted their blood and their rage without being able to arrive at any satisfactory settlement, shall agree at the last extremity to have recourse to the Holy See. Then the Pope shall send to France a special legate…in consequence of the information received, His Holiness himself shall nominate a most Christian King for the government of France.

After the three days of darkness, St. Peter and St. Paul, having come down from Heaven, will preach in the whole world and designate a new Pope. A great light will flash from their bodies and will settle upon the cardinal who is to become Pope. Christianity then will spread throughout the world. He is the Holy Pontiff, chosen by God to withstand the storm. At the end, he will have the gift of miracles, and his name shall be praised over the whole earth. Whole nations will come back to the Church and the face of the earth will be renewed. Russia, England, and China, will come into the Church.

Blessed Anna Maria Taigi predicts wars and revolutions prior to the three days of darkness. We see today many revolutions and unrest throughout the world. Christians are being persecuted and murdered daily especially in the eastern nations.

What is astounding is the current events in France. On November 13, 2015, during a series of coordinated attacks in Paris, 130 people were killed, and approximately 368 were wounded. The majority of the attackers were French citizens. Could this be a start of the civil unrest Blessed Taigi predicts?

In the United States, religion is also being persecuted more intently. Lawsuits are filed over crosses in public places, no praying or mentioning God in public schools or any public arena. This past Christmas it was extremely difficult to find a Christmas card that stated Merry Christmas rather than happy holidays. The secularist and atheist want to exclude God from people as much as possible. Of course we can expect retribution from God the more we exclude him from our lives. God is life, God is one with the universe. God loves us and wants us to share eternal life with him and will send us trials in order for us to remember him.

Blessed Anna Maria Taigi specifically states darkness will be filled with pestilence. Merriam Webster dictionary's definition of pestilence is "a contagious or infectious epidemic disease that is virulent and devastating; specifically: bubonic plague." Ebola, an infectious and currently a generally deadly virus, has killed thousands in West Africa, and now has made its way to other nations. There is no cure for Ebola at this time, but several antibiotics in the testing phase have proved effective. Could this life threatening disease become out of control and coincide with the three days of darkness?

"The air shall be infected by demons who will appear under all sorts of hideous forms." Blessed Anna Maria Taigi's prediction is similar to Revelations 9:1-6: "The sun and the air were darkened by the smoke from the passage. Locusts came out of the earth." The locusts in this prediction are referring to demons. A horrendous thought that demons will appear in hideous forms and be prevalent on earth. Many saints described demons taking the shape of earthly animals to provoke fear. The saints then prayed for assistance and the demons vanished. We must remember to not be afraid but turn to God, Holy Mary, and the saints for assistance and have faith during our prayers!

"He, who out of curiosity, opens his window to look out, or leaves his home, will fall dead on the spot." This prophecy is reminiscent of the destruction of Sodom and Gomorrah in Genesis 19, as the angels said to Lot: "Flee for your life! Do not look back or stop anywhere on the Plain. Flee to the hills at once or you will be swept away." Why were they told not to look back, and why is Blessed Anna Maria Taigi warning us not to look out during the three days of darkness?

In the beginning of her prediction she states evils, revolutions, and wars will originate on earth, but the three days of darkness will come from **heaven**. In the 1981 movie "Raiders of the Lost Ark," directed by Steven Spielberg, there is a scene where the Ark of the Covenant is opened. Ghastly spirits decimate those watching. Indy, played by Harrison Ford, screams to Marion, played by Karen Allen, to close her eyes. After all those present die, Indy and Marion are still alive. Perhaps this scene is relevant to the Bible passage in 1 Samuel 6:19-20: "The descendants of Jeconiah did not join in the celebration with the inhabitants of Beth-shemesh when they saw the ark of the Lord, and seventy of them were struck down. The people mourned over this great calamity which the Lord had inflicted upon them. The men of Beth-shemesh asked, 'Who can stand in the presence of the Lord, this Holy God?'" Was Indy aware of this passage whereby knowing to close his eyes? As in this scene, Blessed Anna Maria Taigi appears to be warning us not to look upon God's anger for his anger is Holy!

The genesis of the predicted three days of darkness is Divine Wrath, as was in the destruction of Sodom and Gomorrah. We know God is merciful and forgiving, but as in our current times when man no longer believes sin is sin, He is capable of being angry with a righteous indignation. "If we sin deliberately after receiving knowledge of the truth, there no longer remains sacrifice for sins but a fearful prospect of judgment and a flaming fire that is going to consume the adversaries." (Hebrews 10; 26-27) God's anger is not irrational but rather a predesigned response to sin. God is Holy, therefore, he can not look upon sin with apathy.

In the book of Romans, Paul writes, "The (Holy) wrath of God is indeed being revealed from heaven against every impiety and wickedness of those who suppress the truth by their wickedness." Paul is advising that all humanity is in a disturbed plight and our Lord's intervention is required in order to be saved. As Blessed Anna Maria Taigi predicts, the three days of darkness will come from heaven as a result of man's sin. Therefore, God's holy wrath during the three days of darkness cannot be looked upon!

The coming three days of darkness was also predicted by Marie Julie Jahenny, a Catholic mystic and stigmatist. She was born February 12, 1850, in Blain, France, and died March 4, 1941. Some say she was one of the greatest mystics the Church has ever known. According to witnesses, because of her piety, she experienced numerous attacks from the devil. She was extremely accurate in predicting World War I and II, various persecutions of the Catholic Church, and more. The last years of her life she was miraculously sustained by the Blessed Host as her only nourishment. She made many prophecies of the future of the Church, the three days of darkness, and the coming of Christ.

On December 14, 1881, Holy Mary spoke to Marie Julie:

> *The time of crimes has begun...the devil will*
>
> *appear in the form of living apparitions...woe to*
>
> *those who dare to make pacts with these*
>
> *personages who appear in diabolical visions...my*
>
> *victim, many souls will be possessed a few months*
>
> *before (the crisis),...the world will be mad with*
>
> *fear and in this madness, the devil who is*

everywhere on earth, will make them deny their

baptism and the cross.

That same day she alluded to abortions that are currently being performed daily in astonishing numbers: "The crimes have begun. Many mothers will be heartless for their own fruits, still innocent, flowers in heaven." From 1973 through 2011, 53 million abortions have been performed. Jones RK and Jerman J, Abortion incidence and service availability in the United States, 2011, Sexual and Reproductive Health, 2014, 46(1):3-14

Stop and think about that number. How could Our Lord, the Creator, not demand justice for the innocents? The apostle Luke tells us Jesus predicted a time when people will say, "Blessed are the barren, the wombs that never bore and the breasts that never nursed." (Luke 23:29) That time is now!

Marie Julie prophecies that at the time of the last crisis:

A large number of souls will be obsessed and

possessed by the infernal spirit and to exorcise

these souls a great number of penances and

mortifications will be required from the Fathers of

the Church that Heaven will subject to this harsh

trial. When the prayer of the Church commands

the infernal spirit to leave, let us never be without

the Cross on us which is the invincible weapon

which overthrows him and forces him to return to

hell.

On June 13, 2014, Pope Francis officially recognized "The International Association of Exorcists." In October 2014, an unprecedented meeting occurred in Rome of more than 300 exorcist from around the world. An official spokesman for the Association, Valter Cascioli M.D., told Vatican Radio, "An increase in occultism and Satanism has opened the door to demonic activity. The number of people taking part in these activities and experiencing serious social, psychological, spiritual and moral damage has been growing. An increase in other demonic phenomena such as vexations, obsessions, and especially diabolical possessions."

An increase in Ouiji board séances and reading witchcraft books has been a cause for concern. These practices **open the door** to demonic activity. Catholic officials are seeing a greater demand for people to talk to them about exorcisms. Father Vince Lambert, one of fifty Vatican trained exorcist in the United States, told International Business Times: "From a faith perspective, it may seem like the devil upped his game so to speak. I don't think the devil has upped his game, but more people are inclined to play that game."

During the October convention, The International Association of Exorcists, discussed the impact of occult and Satanism. Turning away from God, as in not praying and participating in tarot reading, can lead to vexation and obsession by evil spirits. A vexation is described as "when someone has been cursed by black magic which can manifest as physical attacks on a person." Obsession is described as "evil spirits causing inner torment and anxiety." This increase in demonic activity seemingly fulfills Marie Julie's prophecy. The demons released from hell during the three days of darkness may not only roam the earth in hideous forms but also possess human bodies in extraordinary numbers.

On January 4, 1884, Marie-Julie predicted:

The infernal powers will be loosed and will execute all the enemies of God. The earth will become like a vast cemetery. The bodies of the wicked and the just will cover the ground. The famine will be great…everything will be thrown into confusion. The crisis will explode suddenly; the punishments will be shared by all and will succeed one another without interruption. The three days of darkness will be on a Thursday, Friday, and Saturday. Days of the Most Holy Sacrament of the Cross and Our Lady…three days less one night.

Marie-Julie's prophecy: "the infernal powers will be loosed and will execute all the enemies of God," is similar to Blessed Anna Maria Taigi's prediction of the demons being released on earth in hideous forms. "…everything will be thrown into confusion." Where God is absent, confusion prevails. If God is present or if something is good then peace exists. When confusion and chaos are present then it is not of God. When confusion exists, it is of the devil because there is no truth or good in him. There is no peace with the devil.

September 20, 1882- Our Lady announced to Marie-Julie:

The earth will be covered in darkness and hell will be loosed on earth. The thunder and lightning will cause those who have no faith or trust in my Power, to die of fear. During these three days of terrifying darkness, no windows must be opened, because no one will be able to see the earth and the terrible color it will have in those days of punishment without dying at once…The sky will be on fire, the earth will split… During these

three days of darkness let the blessed candle be

lighted everywhere, no other light will shine.

"The sky will be on fire, the earth will split…"
Could this be caused by a comet or great volcanoes?
Another theory is the three days of darkness could be
caused by a magnetic pole shift which occurs when the
north and south poles change places. A drastic increase
in natural disasters and unexplained phenomena have
scientist believing a pole reversal is now taking place.
Extraordinarily, seven volcanoes worldwide have
recently started to erupt (2015), as well as an increase in
earthquake activity measuring over 7.0 magnitude. A
sudden magnetic pole shift could wreak havoc
worldwide causing earthquakes, tsunamis and volcanoes
to erupt.

A volcanic eruption in Yellowstone National Park
would cause a worldwide catastrophe. Scientists are
increasingly more concerned as recent evidence
indicates a volcanic eruption could not only occur from

earthquake activity opening the earth's crust allowing the magma to escape, but also as a result of a build up of pressure. A super volcano eruption like this would cause a "volcanic winter," sulfur dioxide (S02) gas entering the earth's atmosphere limiting sunlight. Although scientist state they don't expect it to erupt in our lifetime, the possibility still exist and this new discovery makes that possibility even greater.

December 8, 1882, she continues:

No one outside a shelter will survive. The earth will shake as at the judgment and fear will be great. Yes, we will listen to the prayers of your friends; Not one will perish. We will need them to publish the glory of the cross.

The candles of blessed wax alone will give light during this horrible darkness. One candle alone will be enough for the duration of this night of hell…In the homes of the wicked and blasphemers

these candles will give no light.

Our Lady continues to Marie-Julie:

Everything will shake except the piece of furniture on which the

blessed candle is burning. This will not shake. You will all gather

around with the crucifix and my blessed picture. This is what will

keep away terror. During this darkness the devils and the wicked

will take on the most hideous shapes…red clouds like blood will

move across the sky. The crash of the thunder will shake the earth

and sinister lightning will streak the heavens out of season. The

earth will be shaken to its foundations. The sea will rise; its

roaring waves will spread over the continent.

October 17, 1883:

> *The wicked will commit all kinds of horrors. The*
>
> *Holy Hosts will be dispersed on the roads. They*
>
> *will be discovered in the mud. The priests as well*

as the faithful will pick them up and will carry

them on their breasts.

December 23, 1881: Marie Julie states:

I understood that the angels would carry away

many tabernacles from the churches to shield the

Holy Sacraments.

Padre Pio is a saint who had the gift of prophecy, who also may have predicted this future tribulation of dark days. St. Pio of Pietrelcina, affectionately known as Padre Pio, was a stigmatist and priest of the Roman Catholic Order of Friars Minor Capuchin. He was born in Pietrelcina, Italy, on May 25, 1887, and died on September 23, 1968. On June 16, 2002, he was canonized by Pope John Paul II. He was known as a man of prayer and prayed unceasingly. On Friday, September 20, 1918, he received the stigmata, the wounds of our Christ, while praying before a crucifix.

A copy of a personal letter (not authenticated) was written by Padre Pio addressed to the Commission of

Heroldsbach. The letter was dated January 28, 1950, and February 7, 1950. Padre Pio foretells the three days of darkness prophecy revealed by God to him:

> *Keep your windows well covered. Do not look out. Light a blessed candle, which will suffice for many days. Pray the rosary. Read spiritual books. Make acts of Spiritual Communion, also acts of love, which are so pleasing to Us. Pray with outstretched arms, or prostrate on the ground, in order that many souls may be saved. Do not go outside the house. Provide yourself with sufficient food. The powers of nature shall be moved and a rain of fire shall make people tremble with fear. Have courage! I am in the midst of you.*

Padre Pio informs us, as the other saints, not to go outside during the chastisement. We should also be prepared for any disaster with ample food, blessed objects, and a blessed candle. He encourages us to pray continually and to be courageous, for God is with us.

He continues:

> *Take care of the animals during these days. I am*
>
> *the Creator and Preserver of all animals as well as*
>
> *man. I shall give you a few signs beforehand, at*
>
> *which time you should place more food before them.*
>
> *I will preserve the property of the elect, including*
>
> *the animals, for they shall be in need of sustenance*
>
> *afterwards as well. Let no one go across the yard,*
>
> *even to feed the animals-he who steps outside will*
>
> *perish! Cover your windows carefully. My elect*
>
> *shall not see My wrath. Have confidence in Me,*
>
> *and I will be your protection. Your confidence*
>
> *obliges Me to come to your aid.*
>
> *The hour of My coming is near! But I will show*

mercy. A most dreadful punishment will bear witness to the times. My angels, who are to be the executioners of this work, are ready with their pointed swords! They will take special care to annihilate all those who mocked Me and would not believe in My revelations.

Hurricanes of fire will pour forth from the clouds and spread over the entire earth! Storms, bad weather, thunderbolts and earthquakes will cover the earth for two days. An uninterrupted rain of fire will take place! It will begin during a very cold night. All this is to prove that God is the Master of Creation. Those who hope in Me, and believe in My words, have nothing to fear because I will not forsake them, nor those who spread My message.

No harm will come to those who are in the state of grace who seek My Mother's protection.

That you may be prepared for these visitations, I will give you the following signs and instructions: That night will be very cold. The wind will roar. After a time, thunderbolts will be heard. Lock all the doors and windows. Talk to no one outside the house. Kneel down before a crucifix, be sorry for your sins, and beg My Mother's protection. Do not look during the earthquake, because the anger of God is holy! Jesus does not want us to behold the anger of God, because God's anger must be contemplated with fear and trembling.

Those who disregard this advice will be killed instantly. The wind will carry with it poisonous gases which will be diffused over the entire earth.

Those who suffer and die innocently will be

martyrs and they will be with Me in My

Kingdom.

In the days of darkness, My elect shall not sleep,

as did the disciples in the garden of olives. They,

shall pray incessantly, and they shall not be

disappointed in Me. I shall gather My elect! Hell

will believe itself to be in possession of the entire

earth, but I shall reclaim it!

Again, Blessed Padre Pio's prediction is similar to the other prophecies. Padre Pio specifically states God's elect shall not see his (Holy) wrath. We will be given signs in the sky to warn us of the impending darkness. He also foretells that the faithful will not sleep during the three days of darkness, and we should pray incessantly.

"The wind will carry with it poisonous gases which will be diffused over the entire earth…" As discussed earlier a super volcano eruption would release sulfur dioxide gas into the stratosphere in biblical proportions. Sulfuric acid droplets are formed when sulfuric dioxide reacts with water. Sulfuric acid along with heavy ash would sicken or kill humans and animals, kill trees and vegetation, and reduce or obscure the sunlight.

Padre Pio states to pray with outstretched hands. Praying in this manner has been known to be very powerful. It symbolizes strength and suffering as well as Jesus suffering on the cross. Praying in this manner goes back as far as Moses in the Old Testament. In the book of Exodus, Chapter 17, during the battle of Amalek, as long as Moses kept his arms raised up, Israel prevailed and later defeated Amalek.

The sixth way of prayer of St. Dominic (1170-1221), as written by an anonymous writer in "The Nine Ways of Prayer of St. Dominic," describes Saint Dominic praying, standing erect with his hands and arms outstretched, forcefully, in the form of a cross. This form of prayer moves God, as the devout pray in unison with his Son suffering on the Cross. We should pray in this manner as much as possible for the perfection of our soul. Our Lord while hanging on the cross with outstretched arms, "offered prayers and supplications with loud cries and tears……he was heard because of his reverence." (Hebrews 5:7)

Blessed Anne Catherine Emmerich also predicted the coming of a great tribulation. She was born in Flamske, Germany, on September 8th, 1774, and died at the age of 49 on February 9th, 1824. She became a nun at the Convent of Agnetenberg at Dulmen on November 13th, 1803. "Although of simple education, she had perfect consciousness of her earliest days and could understand the liturgical Latin from her first time at Mass." As other saints before her, she bore the stigmata of Our Lord, including the crown of thorns and a cross over her heart.

Her biography, as stated in the book, "The life of Jesus Christ and Biblical Revelations," describes her: "During most of her later years she would vomit up even the simplest food or drink, subsisting for long periods almost entirely on water and the Holy Eucharist. She was told in a mystic vision that her gift of seeing past, present, and future was greater than that possessed by anyone else in history." So detailed were her prophecies of Jesus' life that the movie "The Passion of Christ" directed by Mel Gibson was based on her revelations.

Catherine Emmerich described in detail the last home of the Blessed Virgin Mary after the death of Jesus Christ. In 1891, a team of researchers followed her detailed description to the ancient city of Ephesus, in Western Turkey, where they located a small stone house that was already honored by local residents. In 1979, Pope John Paul II declared the house a place of worship. Thousands visit the site yearly as a pilgrimage, and is honored in particular, on the feast of the Assumption.

One noteworthy vision Catherine experienced revealed the location of Adam's bones: "I saw Adam's bones reposing in a cavern under Mt. Calvary deep down, almost to water level, and in a straight line beneath the spot on which Jesus was crucified. I looked in and saw Adam's skeleton entire with the exception of the right arm and foot and a part of the right side."

Anne Catherine's prophecies, March 22, 1820:

> *I saw very clearly the errors the aberrations and*
>
> *the countless sins of men. I saw the folly and the*
>
> *wickedness of their actions, against all truth and*

all reason. Priests were among them, and I gladly

endured my suffering so that they may return to a

better mind.

April 12, 1820:

I had another vision of the great tribulation. It

seems to me that a concession was demanded from

the clergy which could not be granted. I saw many

older priests, especially one, who wept bitterly. A

few younger ones were also weeping. But others,

and the lukewarm among them, readily did what

was demanded. It was as if people were splitting

into two camps.

May 13, 1820:

I saw also the relationship between the two

popes…I saw how baleful would be the

consequences of this false church. I saw it increase

in size; heretics of every kind came into the city (of

Rome). The local clergy grew lukewarm, and I saw

a great darkness... Then the vision seemed to

extend on every side. Whole Catholic communities

were being oppressed, harassed, confined, and

deprived of their freedom. I saw many churches

closed down, great miseries everywhere, wars and

bloodshed. A wild and ignorant mob took violent

action. But it did not last long...

Once more I saw that the Church of Peter was

undermined by a plan evolved by the secret sect,

while storms were damaging it. But I saw also that

help was coming when distress had reached its

peak. I saw again the Blessed Virgin ascend on

the Church and spread her mantle (over it). I saw

a Pope who was at once gentle and very firm.... I

saw a great renewal, and the Church rose high in

the sky.

It was previously suggested the two popes in this prophecy may predict a future anti-pope, but it also could refer to our current Pope Francis and retired Pope Benedict. Catherine Emmerich does not elaborate what relationship they possess. Many churches have closed down throughout the nation and Christians are being persecuted for their faith especially in the Islam dominated regions. As predicted, there is hope after the distress has reached its peak. We must continually pray!

Catherine Emmerich predictions continue, July, 1820:

I saw the Holy Father surrounded by traitors and in great

distress about the Church. He had visions and apparitions

in his hour of greatest need. I saw many good pious

Bishops; but they were weak and wavering, their cowardice

often got the upper hand…Then I saw darkness spreading

around and people no longer seeking the true Church.

July 12, 1820:

Although there was no altar bell, the cruets were

there. The wine was as red as blood, and there was

also some water. The Mass was short. The Gospel

of St. John was not read at the end.

August 25, 1820:

I do not know in what manner I was taken to

Rome last night, but I found myself near the

Church of St Mary Major, and I saw many poor

people who were greatly distressed and worried

because the Pope was to be seen nowhere, and also

on account of the restlessness and the alarming

rumors in the city. These people did not seem to

expect the Church doors to open; they only wanted

to pray outside. An inner urging had left them there individually. But I was in the Church, and I opened the doors. They came in, surprised and frightened because the doors had opened. It seems me to that I was behind the door, and they could not see me. There was no office in the Church. But the sanctuary lamps were lit. The people prayed quite peacefully. Then I saw an apparition of the Mother of God, and she said that the tribulation would be very great. She added that people must pray fervently with outstretched arms, be it only long enough to say three Our Fathers. This was the way her Son prayed for them on the Cross. They must rise at twelve at night, and pray in this manner; and they must keep coming to the Church. They must pray above all for the Church of Darkness to leave Rome. She (The Holy

Mother) said a great many others things that it pains me to relate: she said that if only one priest could offer the bloodless sacrifice as worthily and with the same disposition as the Apostles, he could avert all the disasters (that are to come). To my knowledge the people in the Church did not see the apparition, but they must have been stirred by something supernatural, because as soon as the Holy Virgin had said that they must pray God with outstretched arms, they all raised their arms. These were all good and devout people, and they did not know where help and guidance should be sought. There were no traitors and enemies among them, yet they were afraid of one another. One can judge thereby what the situation was like.

September 10, 1820:

I saw the Church of St Peter: it has been destroyed

but for the Sanctuary and the main Altar. St

Michael came down into the Church, clad in his

suit of armor, and he paused, threatening with his

sword and number of unworthy pastors who

wanted to enter. That part of the Church, which

had been destroyed, was promptly fenced in with

light timber, so that the Divine office might be

celebrated as it should. Then, from all over the

world came priests and laymen and they rebuilt the

stone walls, since the wreckers had been unable to

move the heavy foundation stones. And then I saw

that the Church was being promptly rebuilt and

She was more magnificent than ever before.

September 12, 1820:

I saw a strange church being built against every

rule. No angels were supervising the building

operations. In that church, nothing came from high above…There was only division and chaos. It is the latest fashion, as well as the new heterodox Church of Rome, which seems of the same kind. I saw again the strange big church that was being built there (in Rome). There was nothing holy in it. …All in this church belonged to the earth, returned to the earth. All was dead, the work of human skill, a church of the latest style, a church of man's invention like the new heterodox church in Rome."

October 7, 1820:

As I was going through Rome with St. Francoise and the other saint, we saw a great palace engulfed in flames from top to bottom. I was very much afraid that the occupants would be burned to death because no one came forward to put out the fire.

As we came nearer, however, the fire abated and we saw the blackened building. We went through a number of magnificent rooms (untouched by the fire), and we finally reached the Pope. He was sitting in the dark and slept in a large arm-chair. He was very ill and weak; he could no longer walk. The ecclesiastics in the inner circle looked insincere and lacking in zeal; I did not like them. I told the Pope of the bishops who are to be appointed soon. I told him also that he must not leave Rome. If he did so, it would be chaos. He thought that the evil was inevitable and that he should leave in order to save many things beside himself. He was very much inclined to leave Rome, and he was insistently urged to do so. The Pope is still attached to the things of this earth in many ways. The Church is completely isolated and as if completely deserted. It seems that everyone is running away. Everywhere I see great misery, hatred, treason, rancor, confusion and utter blindness. O city! O city! What is threatening thee? The storm is coming, do be watchful!

April 22, 1823

I saw that many pastors allowed themselves to be taken up with ideas that were dangerous to the Church. They were building a great, strange, and extravagant Church. Everyone was to be admitted in it in order to be united and have equal rights: Evangelicals, Catholics, sects of every description. Such was to be the new Church...But God had other designs. I see that when the Second Coming of Christ approaches, a bad priest will do much harm to the Church. When the time of the reign of Antichrist is near, a false religion will appear which will be opposed to the unity of God and His

Church. This will cause the greatest schism the

world has ever known. The nearer the time of the

end, the more the darkness of Satan will spread on

earth, the greater will be the number of the children

of corruption, and the number of the just will

correspondingly diminish…

Was Catherine Emmerich referring to the changes that were made with the Second Vatican Council (1962-1965) as the "Dark Church?" Many would believe so. In the book, "The Spirit of the Liturgy," by Joseph Cardinal Ratzinger (Pope Benedict), the Cardinal examines the misinterpretation of the intentions of the Second Vatican Council. "I am simply offering an aid to the understanding of the faith and the right way to give the faith its central form of expression in the Liturgy." He discusses the present Liturgical deficiencies and unintended changes, such as the location of the tabernacle, the posture of kneeling, music during the Liturgy, and the orientation of prayer during the Mass. Cardinal Ratzinger states: "The fresco was laid bare by the Liturgical Movement and, in a definitive way, by the Second Vatican Council. For a moment its colors and figures fascinated us. But, since then the fresco has been endangered by climatic conditions, as well as by various restorations and reconstructions. In fact, it is threatened with destruction, if the necessary steps are not taken to stop these damaging influences. Of course, there must be no question of its being covered with whitewash again, but what is imperative is a new reverence in the way we treat it, a new understanding of its message and its reality, so that rediscovery does not become the first state of irreparable loss."

St. Hildegard also predicted the three days of darkness. St. Hildegard was born around 1098, in West Franconia, Germany, and died on September 17, 1179. St. Hildegard was a Benedictine abbess, a German writer, a mystic/visionary, composer, and philosopher. Pope Benedict XVI, on October 7, 2012, named her a Doctor of the Church. St. Hildegard predicted a great tribulation:

A powerful wind will rise in the north carrying heavy fog and the densest of dust by divine command, and it will fill their throats and eyes so that they will cease their savagery and be stricken with a great fear. Before the comet comes, many nations, the good accepted, will be scourged by want and famine. The great nation that is in the ocean that is inhabited by people of different tribes and descent will be devastated by an (sic.) earthquake, storm, and tidal wave. It will be divided and, in great part, submerged. That nation will also have many misfortunes at sea and lose its colonies. By its tremendous pressure the comet will force much out of the ocean and flood many countries, causing much want and many plagues. All coastal cities will live in fear, and many of them will be destroyed by tidal waves, and most living creatures will be killed, and even those who

escape will die from horrible diseases. For in none

of those cities does a person live according to the

laws of God.

St. Hildegard specifically predicts a comet will hit the earth causing great floods. A normal tsunami is generally caused by an earthquake, or movement of the sea floor generating waves that have a small wave off shore, and a very long wavelength that increase in height when it reaches shore. In contrast, a mega tsunami is caused by an impact event such as a comet crashing into the ocean. This would result in a massive water displacement, causing waves thousands of feet high that would transverse oceans and land, causing unparalleled global destruction.

Many of the prophecies of the three days of darkness refer to a comet impacting the earth. It is feasible that such an event could immerse the earth in a cloud of dust causing a period of darkness.

Additional noteworthy predictions:

"He who survives those three days of darkness and horror will see himself as if alone, because the earth will be covered with cadavers." St Gasper del Bufalo (d. 1837)

"There shall be three days of darkness, during which the atmosphere will be infected by innumerable devils, who will cause the death of large multitudes of unbelievers and wicked men. Blessed candles alone shall be able to give light and preserve the faithful Catholics from the impending, dreadful scourge. Supernatural prodigies will appear in the heavens…" Sister Palma Maria of Oria, Italy (d. 1863)

"During a darkness lasting three days the people given to evil will perish so that only one fourth of mankind will survive." Sister Mary of Jesus Crucified of Pau (d. 1878) later beatified in 1983 by Pope John Paul II

"There will come three days of continuous darkness. Only blessed candles will give some light during this horrible darkness. One candle will last three days, but they will not give light in the houses of the Godless. Lightning will penetrate your houses, but it will not put out the blessed candles. Neither wind, nor storm, nor earthquake will put out the blessed candles. Red clouds, like blood, will cross the sky, and the crash of thunder will shake the earth to its very core. The ocean will cast its foaming waves over the land, and the earth will be turned into a huge graveyard. The bodies of the wicked and of the righteous will cover the face of the earth. The famine that follows will be severe. All plant life will be destroyed as well as three fourths of the human race. This crisis will be sudden and the punishment will be world wide." The French nun, Marie de la Faudais (1819)

"For seven days the great star shall be seen, as if two suns in the sky should appear, the big Mastiff shall be howling all night,

when the Pontiff should go into exile...During the time the hairy star appears (comet), struck from heaven, shaky piece, shaking earth (earthquakes)...new downpour, sudden, impetuous, unexpected, shall hinder two armies, Stone, Heaven, Fire, shall fall over the sea..." Nostradamus-Michel de Nostredame (d.1566)

In 1976, while addressing the Eucharistic Congress in Philadelphia, then Cardinal Wojtyla (Pope John Paul II), made a predictive statement: "We are now standing in the face of the greatest historical confrontation humanity has ever experienced. I do not think the wide circle of the American society, or the wide circle of the Christian community, realize this fully. We are now facing the final confrontation between the Church and the anti-Church, between the Gospel and the anti-Gospel, between Christ and the Antichrist. This confrontation lies within the plans of Divine Providence. It is therefore within God's plans and must be a trial which the Church must take up and face courageously."

II

Punishment and Prophecy in the Bible

God is the Supreme Judge of us all. God will determine our fate at the time of death based on how we lived our lives. But, keep in account God is merciful to us all. No sin is too great that God cannot forgive even at the last second when we take our last breath. We were created to serve him, and he sends us trials to remember him and repent, so that when we die we may share in his presence. So, what other way can God get our attention than to send us these calamities as we see throughout the Bible? What will it take to wake us up and leave our life of sin? Does Sacred Scripture predict the three days of darkness?

As we have seen in the Old Testament, God dispenses his judgment not only on individuals, but on nations. God, who is unchanging, is the judge and punisher of nations, now, just as in the Old Testament.

Sin appears exceedingly rampant in every nation as we see Christians being murdered for their faith, mutilation, abortion, murder, rape, abuse and sexual crimes against children, excessive greed, perverse music, self-indulgence, and drugs and alcohol abuse. We hear of these atrocities occurring daily as if the nations are spiraling out of control. How can we expect to live each day in sin with no retribution by God? If God is unchanging, can we not expect him to dispense his judgment on a sinful nation now as in the Old Testament?

God judged the angels when they sinned, as evident in the angels who came to the earth and had relations with the women: "The angel too, who did not keep to their own domain but deserted their proper dwelling, he has kept in eternal chains, in gloom, for the judgment of the great day."(Jude 1: 6) In "Lessons from the Past" (2 Peter 2: 4-10) God's judgment is evident: *"For if God did not spare the angels when they sinned, but condemned them to the chains of Tartarus and handed them over to be kept for judgment; and if he did not spare the ancient world, even though he preserved Noah, a herald of righteousness, together with seven others, when he brought a flood upon the godless world;*

and if he condemned the cities of Sodom and Gomorrah (to destruction), reducing them to ashes, making them an example for the godless (people) of what is coming; and if he rescued Lot, a righteous man oppressed by the licentious conduct of unprincipled people (for day after day that righteous man living among them was tormented in his righteous soul at the lawless deeds that he saw and heard), then the Lord knows how to rescue the devout from trial and to keep the unrighteous under punishment for the day of judgment, and especially those who follow the flesh with its depraved desire and show contempt for lordship."

We can also see God dispensing his judgment in the "Plagues of Egypt;" the ninth plague being darkness. *"Then the Lord said to Moses: 'Stretch out your hand toward the sky, that over the land of Egypt there should be such darkness that one can feel it.' So Moses stretched out his hand toward the sky, and there was dense darkness throughout the land of Egypt for three days."*(Exodus 10: 21-22) Again, we see the punishment of darkness occurred for three days! It's also worth reiterating that the darkness was so thick it could be felt.

God disciplines us because he loves us. God wants us to spend eternal salvation with him. In order for us to merit Heaven, he must send us trials and punishments to expiate our sins. *"You have also forgotten the exhortation addressed to you as sons: 'My son, do not disdain the discipline of the Lord or lose heart when reproved by him; for whom the Lord loves, he disciplines; he scourges every son he acknowledges.' Endure your trials as "discipline"; God treats you as sons. For what "son" is there whom his father does not discipline? If you are without discipline, in which all have shared, you are not sons but bastards. Besides this, we have had our earthly fathers to discipline us, and we respected them. Should we not (then) submit all the more to the Father of spirits and live? They disciplined us for a short time as seemed right to them, but He does so for our benefit, in order that we may share his holiness. At the time, all discipline seems a cause not for joy but for pain, yet later it brings the peaceful fruit of righteousness to those who are trained by it."* (Hebrews 12: 5-11)

Will a great earthquake precede the three days of darkness as predicted? We see in the Bible seismic activity as a sign of God's anger and disappointment as we read at the time of Jesus' death: *"And behold, the veil of the sanctuary was torn in two from top to bottom. The earth quaked, rocks were split, tombs were opened, and the bodies of many saints who had fallen asleep were raised."* (Matthew 27: 51-54)

Some may dispute natural events, such as earthquakes, are ordinary scientific earthly occurrences. Obviously, not all earthquakes are a sign of God's anger. This may be true, but how can we dispute that "great" earthquakes may also be a warning from God. For we see in the Bible at the time of Jesus' death a great earthquake occurred. Is this just a coincidence? God and nature are one, God and earth are one! The sin of people infect the earth, for God and creation are one. When we sin we corrupt both others and nature. Evil will infect the earth. David writes, "The earth rocked and shook; the foundations of the mountains trembled; they shook as his wrath flared up." (Psalm 18: 8) The earth trembling is also a sign or warning from God and not just old folklore.

Does the Bible predict the three days of darkness? *"Then the fifth angels blew his trumpet, and I saw a star that had fallen from the sky to the earth. It was given the key for the passage to the abyss. It opened the passage to the abyss, and smoke came up out of the passage like smoke from a huge furnace. The sun and the air were darkened by the smoke from the passage. Locusts came out of the earth. They were told not to harm the grass of the earth or any plant or any tree, but only those people who did not have the seal of God on their foreheads. They were not allowed to kill them but only to torment them for five months the torment they inflicted was like that of a scorpion when it stings a person. During that time these people will seek death but will not find it, and they will long to die but death will escape them."* (Revelation 9: 1-6)

As predicted, many seers say a comet or something will fall from the sky prior to the three days of darkness. This will be a sign and a warning that the three days of darkness will commence. Does this passage in Revelation make this same prediction? The passage states this "star" will open the abyss causing smoke to darken the sky. The smoke meaning the darkness that will envelope the earth. The locusts being the demons who will come out of the earth to torment us as predicted by so many.

We read in Isaiah another passage that seemingly predicts the coming three days of darkness. *"Indeed, the day of the Lord comes, cruel, with wrath and burning anger; To lay waste the land and destroy the sinners within it! The stars of the heavens and their constellations will send forth no light; The sun will be dark at its rising, and the moon will not give its light. Thus I will punish the world for its evil and the wicked for their guilt. I will put an end to the pride of the arrogant, the insolence of tyrants I will humble. I will make mortals more rare than pure gold, human beings, than the gold of Ophir. For this I will make the heavens tremble and the earth shall be shaken from its place, At the wrath of the Lord of hosts on the day of his burning anger."* (Isaiah 13: 9-13) Again, we hear God's anger and displeasure evident in an earthquake.

There are more passages in the Bible that appear to describe days of darkness and the coming of the day of the Lord. *"It shall come to pass I will pour out my spirit upon all fresh. Your sons and daughters will prophesy, your old men will dream dreams, your young men will see visions. Even upon your male and female servants, in those days, I will pour out my spirit. I will set signs in the heavens and on the earth, blood, fire, and columns of smoke; The sun will darken, the moon turn blood-red, Before the day of the Lord arrives, that great and terrible day. Then everyone who calls upon the name of the Lord will escape harm."* (Joel 3: 1-5)

You hear more and more recently how people are having dreams of future catastrophes or just a "feeling" of impending disasters. The signs in the sky correlate with the predictions of a "warning" before the three days of darkness occur. God will give time to those who heed his warning and prepare. Again, as in the previous passages we hear of smoke and darkness. We also see in the last sentence that everyone who calls upon the name of the Lord will escape harm. We must have faith in Him and His mercy to all who believe and ask forgiveness.

Another passage in the Bible predicts days of darkness: *"Immediately after the tribulation of those days, the sun will be darkened, and the moon will not give its light and the stars will fall from the sky, and the powers of the heavens will be shaken."* (Matthew 24: 29-30)

We also read in Luke the same prophecy: *"There will be signs in the sun, the moon and the stars, and on earth nations will be in dismay, perplexed by the roaring of the sea and the waves. People will die of fright in anticipation of what is coming upon the world, for the powers of the heavens will be shaken."* These prophecies are to occur prior to the coming of the Son on Man.

Another passage in Revelations describes the sun being darkened: *"Then I watched while he broke open the sixth seal, and there was a great earthquake; the sun turned as black as dark sackcloth and the whole moon became like blood. The stars in the sky fell to the earth like unripe figs shaken loose from the tree in a strong wind. Then the sky was divided like a torn scroll curling up, and every mountain and island was moved from its place."*

In this passage the sun may be darkened by smoke or volcanic activity. The earthquake will cause great fires. The smoke will darken the skies and the moon will look red.

On July 24, 2014, the tomb of Jonah was destroyed by ISIS (Islamic State in Iraq and Syria) militants. These militants planted explosives around the tomb and detonated them completely destroying the holy site. This was a pilgrimage site for Christians and Jews.

Jonah spent three days in the belly of the whale, and was significant in predicting that Jesus would spend three days in darkness prior to his resurrection. Is this a sign of the impending three days of darkness as well? Could the destruction of Jonah's tomb be a turning point in history?

III

The Significance of the Number Three

Why would the prophecy of the three days of darkness last only three days and not one or seven days? Is the number three God's special number? Does the number three have a spiritual significance? Why would God allow Jesus to die on the cross for three hours, and remain in darkness for three days? From nature to the scriptures to symbolism, it appears the number three is a divine number and a significant reference to life itself.

The number three could be considered a sign of completeness. The triangle is not complete without the third line, otherwise two straight lines cannot enclose any space. Three dimensions are necessary to form a solid object consisting of length, width, and height. The three kingdoms that embrace matter are mineral, vegetable, and matter. Time is divided into three: past, present, and future. The sum of human capability is thought, word, and deed. There are three phases in life: birth, life, and death. A complete man is formed with body, soul, and spirit. Therefore, the number three represents completeness, oneness, something substantial, in entirety.

As related to Scriptures, this completeness transcends to Divinity. The number three is divine and becomes a numerical signature of God. God's attributes are three: Omniscience, Omnipresence, and Omnipotence. The dogma of the Trinity teaches us that the Trinity is a term used to signify there are three persons; the Father, the Son, and the Holy Spirit in One God.

The number three has been long been symbolized in Christian art. St. Patrick used the three leaf clover to represent the Holy Trinity. Many Pope's used the three crowned Tiara in their coat of arms, also representing The Blessed Trinity. The three spiked Fleur de Lis was used as an emblem of the King of France. The Fleur de Lis represented the Trinity or The Blessed Virgin Mary and was used by St. Joan of Arc as a coat of arms. The US Army uses the Fleur de Lis on insignia to represent bravery and integrity.

The number three is also prevalent in the dedication of Catholic churches. Individual churches are known by their dedication to a saint or a mystery. These dedications fall into three classes: memorial, proprietary, and personal. A memorial dedication is where a church is erected on the site of martyrdom, or a burial of a saint. A proprietary dedication is a dedication to the founder of the church. Lastly, a personal dedication is a dedication reflecting a devotion of a founder or patron, as to Our Lady or saints like St. Joseph or St. Michael. The personal dedication is the most common.

Three connotes divine perfection, and is prevalent in heaven as well. The choir of Angels is divided into three triads containing nine orders. The first triads are the Angels, Archangels, and Principalities. The mission of these angels is to watch over the universe and specific interests, including the wellbeing of people. Each human being, each church, and each country has a guardian angel.

The second triads of angels are the Powers, Virtues, and Dominations. These angels are known as the "angels of creation," because they are assigned to govern the universe and the majority of causes.

The third triad is the Thrones, Cherabim, and Seraphim. They contemplate the Glory of God. Nearest to the throne of God are the seven wing seraphim, who burn most with the love of God, singing the Sanctus, "Holy, Holy, Holy, Lord God of Hosts" (Isaiah 6:3)

We find the number three prevalent in the teachings of the Catholic Church. As previously discussed, the Trinity consists of God, Son, and Holy Spirit. However, we find the number three also in other teachings. For instance, three conditions must be met for a sin to be mortal; Sin who's object is (1) grave matter, (2) committed with full knowledge, and (3) deliberate consent.

The Catholic catechism also teaches the three powers of the soul; memory, intellect, and will. Also taught are the three pillars of the Church's authority; Sacred Scripture, Sacred Tradition, and Living Magisterium. The three duties of the ordained; duty to teach (based on Christ's role as prophet), duty to sanctify (based on Christ's role as priest), and duty to shepherd (based on Christ's role as King).

There are the three parts of the Catholic Church; the church militant (Christians on earth), the church suffering (Christians in purgatory), and the church triumphant (Christians in Heaven). There are also three levels of reverence; the reverence we give to saints, the reverence we give to Mary as the greatest of saints and the Mother of God, and the reverence and worship we give to God alone.

The use of the number three and its form occurs hundreds of times in both the Old and New Testament of the Bible. What appears most significant in the Bible is how the number three pertains to Jesus and his death and resurrection.

At the beginning of life, Jesus is one member of The Holy Family consisting of three: Joseph, Mary, and Jesus. Three wise men brought gifts for Jesus to pay him homage. After three years of preaching, Jesus was crucified at the age of 33, "When Jesus began his ministry he was about thirty years of age."(Luke 3:23). During his ministry Jesus raised three people from the dead, the widow's son at Nain (Luke 7:13-15), Jairus' daughter (Matthew 9:25), and Lazarus (John 11:43-44)

While Jesus was fasting in the desert, Satan tempted him three times, and Jesus responded by citing three Scriptural passages. (Mathew 4:1-6) Peter denied

Jesus three times before the cock crowed. (Luke 23: 54-61) He was also one of three who was crucified on Mount Calvary that day. (Luke 23:33) Jesus spent three hours in darkness: "It was now about noon and darkness came over the whole land until three in the afternoon because of an eclipse of the sun." (Luke 23:44) Jesus resurrected on the third day: "that he was buried; that he was raised on the third day in accordance with the Scriptures." (1 Corinthians 15:4)

Jesus' resurrection on the third day correlates with the beginning of time. On the third day, in the Story of Creation: "Then God said: Let there be lights in the dome of the sky, to separate day from night." (Genesis 1:13-15)

It could be concluded that three is a number of "Resurrection!" "Come, let us return to the Lord, for it is he who has torn, but he will heal us; he has struck down, but he will bind our wounds. He will revive us after two days; On the third day he will raise us up, to live in his presence."(Hosea 6:1-2) "Behold, I cast out demons and I perform healings today and tomorrow, and on the third day I accomplish my purpose." (Luke 14:3)

The spiritual significance of the number three is evident in the prophecies of the coming days of darkness. No other number would be as apropos, for after this chastisement a new beginning will ensue with a period of peace.

IV

Spiritual and Material Darkness

Merriam-Webster's definition of dark is: "devoid or partially devoid of light; dismal and gloomy; unenlightened; not clear to the understanding; relating to grim or depressing circumstances."

Have you ever experienced true darkness? Darkness can be described in two forms both materially or spiritually. Hiding in a dark closet you may feel that it's as dark as it could be. But in reality, a small amount of light always makes its way through the dark, whether it is a minuscule amount from the moon, or a light from another room, however slight. A noteworthy place to visit is the Crystal Caverns located in the Sequoia National Park in California. As you enter the caverns the walls are illuminated by lights supplied by the park. Deeper into the caverns the park attendant closes all the lights and you experience the darkest dark. If you placed your hand a couple inches in front of your face you still can not see it. A sense of deep appreciation for light envelopes you as the lights are then turned back on.

Many children and some adults fear the dark. Could there be a monster or unknown evil waiting in the dark of the night to pounce on you? Perhaps the dark itself is not feared, but the fear of the unknown, or potential, or imagined dangers concealed by the dark. Doesn't the child show a sign of relief when the light is turned on or the sun rises?

We know that criminals use the concealment of the darkness to accomplish their evil deeds. "And this is the verdict, that the light came into the world, but people preferred darkness to light, so that his works might not be exposed. But whoever lives the truth comes to the light, so that his works may be clearly seen as done in God." (John 3; 19-21) "The way of the wicked is like darkness; they do not know on what they stumble." (Proverbs 4; 19)

The Bible, divinely inspired, is the best source of information while investigating the spiritual significance of darkness. God makes light and darkness. "I am the Lord, there is no other. I form the light, and create the darkness, I make weal and create woe; I the Lord, do all these things."(Isaiah 45: 7)

In this following passage, we know that God not only creates good, but utilizes evil to accomplish his will. "See, I have created the smith who blows on the burning coals and forges weapons as his work; It is I also who have created the destroyer to work havoc."(Isaiah 54: 16) God uses evil people and dark events to accomplish his ultimate goal or will.

The Bible Dictionary in the New American Bible describes darkness as "Absence of light." In the Bible, God, who is eternal truth, is considered the true light and the source of all light. (Isaiah 10: 17) Therefore, darkness becomes a symbol of estrangement from God. Jesus said that those who followed him would not walk in darkness. (John 8; 12) He clearly would show them the truth.

In our current busy times more and more people don't take the time to pray and have quiet contemplation with God. We find ourselves waking in the morning checking our smart phones or computers for emails or messages, and throughout the day spending more time watching television. God is the

light and the truth, and without God darkness spreads
and increases. "And they will look to the earth, but
behold, distress and darkness, the gloom of anguish.
And they will be thrust into thick darkness." (Isaiah 8:
22) Undoubtedly, the lack of prayer and the Light (God)
will manifest into a complete darkness as predicted, so
all may recognize God as the Supreme Light of the
World. Notice the adjective "thick" to describe the
darkness. A mental picture of the extent of the darkness
over the earth can be envisioned.

David writes in Psalm 18: 12-14: "He made
darkness his cloak around him; his canopy, water-
darkened storm-clouds. From the gleam before him, his
clouds passed, hail and coals of fire. The Lord
thundered from heaven; the Most High made his voice
resound." The Lord uses darkness as a sign and warning
from heaven throughout the Bible.

Many saints experienced what is called "a darkness
of the soul." Saints such as St. Theresa of Lisieux, St.
John of the Cross, and Blessed Teresa of Calcutta
(Mother Teresa), experienced a terrifying period of
darkness of the soul, that lasted either a short amount
of time, or even months or years. St. Theresa of Lisieux,

The Little Flower, stated to her sisters in the convent, "If only you knew what darkness I am plunged into."

Theresa suffered from tuberculosis, and through this sickness she experienced dark nights of the soul. She continued to be faithful to God and trust in his merciful love. God allowed her to experience this feeling of abandonment, so that she may grow spiritually and trust in him.

St. John of the Cross (1542-1591), described these intense desolation feelings in a poem, "Dark Night of the Soul." He describes the journey of the soul from the "dark night" to the "divine union of the love of God." St. John not only describes his journey, but appears to comfort and encourage the readers, as they experience this same struggle with the desolating dark night.

In the private letters and journals of Mother Teresa, she describes a period of decades in which she felt God was not with her. "In my soul I feel just that terrible pain of loss of God not wanting me- of God not being God- of God not existing." Even through these feelings of being alone, she lived a life dedicated to God, and exemplified his love.

Have you ever felt lonely or afraid without spiritual guidance? Even after prayer you feel as if God is not with you, and you feel anxiety, and spiritually lost. Why does God allow us to have this darkness of the soul and especially the saints who we would imagine have a special place with God? This desolation by God in reality is a time of spiritual growth. Life is not without trials, and through these experiences we learn to rely and trust more in God.

A psalm of David, Psalm 13, describes the desolation David felt and ultimately the trust and mercy he felt from God:

"How long, Lord? Will you utterly forget me?

How long will you hide your face from me?

How long must I carry sorrow in my soul?

Grief in my heart day after day?

How long will my enemy triumph over me?

Look upon me, answer me, Lord, my God!

Give light to my eyes lest I sleep in death,

Lest my enemy say, "I have prevailed,"

Lest my foes rejoice at my downfall.

But I trust in your mercy.

Grant my heart joy in your salvation,

I will sing to the Lord,

For he has dealt bountifully with me!"

The number three is associated with darkness. As in creation, on the third day the light was created, Jesus was in darkness for three days before rising, and Jonah was in the darkness of the belly of the whale for three days. We can clearly calculate, based on Bible literature, why the prediction of the three days of darkness could be forthcoming as predicted. These three days of darkness is described as a material darkness, but may also be a spiritual darkness where we will be tested by God to trust in him!

V

Demon's Released from Hell

During the three days of darkness, it was predicted that the demons would be released from hell to wreak havoc upon the earth. These demons were predicted to be visible in hideous forms. Many saints throughout history have seen demons taking the form of a deformed creature or some form of animal. The mystics and saints suffered in union with Christ to save souls, and the devil would take on hideous forms to torment the saint for this reason.

The devil, knowing the saint could save a soul from damnation, works aggressively with all the powers of hell. Normally, for most people, the devil works secretly to tempt us. We would be horrified to see a demon as a vicious creature, and the devil knows it would work against him. So he chooses to tempt us secretly. "Satan's greatest triumph is to convince the world he does not exist." For if we were to see the demon in this horrific way, we would turn from sin. But for these victim souls, more extreme measures were needed. The demons would continually attack them spiritually and sometimes physically assaulting them. Their intention is to cause despair and distrust in God. The devil felicitates despair or confusion, because he is fully aware he can easily influence a despondent soul to turn away from God's merciful love. During the three days of darkness, Satan will work aggressively to gain as many souls as possible, knowing his time nears the end.

Saint Gemma Galgani (d.1903), was one saint who experienced such horrific occurrences with the devil. A descriptive detail of her experiences can be found in the article, "The Life of Gemma Galgani," by Venerable Father Germanus C.P. In a letter to Father Germanus, Gemma tells him Jesus had told her, "My daughter, the devil will soon wage a war against you." In the letter she begs the Father to pray for her and expresses her concern if she will win this battle with the devil. She later learns the best weapon against the devil is continuous prayer. The devil attempted to prevent her from praying by trying to upset her, or causing her to have intense headaches so she would go to bed rather than pray. Gemma once said, *"Oh, what torment this gives me, not to be able to pray! What fatigue it costs me! How many efforts does not that wretch make to make it impossible for me to pray! Yesterday evening he tried to kill me, and would have succeeded if Jesus had not come quickly to my aid. I was terrified and kept the image of Jesus in my mind, but I could not pronounce his name."*

Gemma also described the devil as taking the shape of a hideous hairy ape type man, or sometimes in the form of a big black dog, grabbing her by the hair, and ripping her from her bed. Another time in her diary she writes: *"Today I thought I was to be entirely free from that nauseous animal, and instead he has knocked me about greatly. I had gone to bed with the full intention of sleeping, but it turned out otherwise. He began to beat me with such blows that I feared I would die. He was in the shape of a big black dog, and he put his "paws" on my shoulders, hurting me greatly. I felt it so much in all my bones that I thought that they were broken. Also, when I was taking holy water he wrenched my arm so violently that I fell to the floor from the pain. The bone was dislocated, but went back into place because Jesus touched it for me, and all was remedied."*

Several of the prophets who predicted the three days of darkness, described demons taking the form of people we know, to trick us during the tribulation. St. Gemma also experienced this type of phenomenon. The devil went so far as to disguise himself as her spiritual director.

Gemma writes that at one time she went to church to make her confession and noticed that the priest was already in the confessional. She felt uneasy, as normally what happened when she was near the devil, but entered the confessional regardless. She stated the priest looked and sounded like her confessor, however his manner of speaking was foul and scandalous. She trembled, and was so disturbed by his behavior, she ran out of the confessional only to realize the pretended priest disappeared. She realized it was the devil attempting to deceive her and cause her to lose faith in her confessor.

In Father Germanus' own biography he writes: *"With a view to protect her from these Satanic attacks and apparitions, I enjoined on her, under whatever form the persons of the other world might appear to her, to at once repeat the words 'Viva Gesu!' (Long live Jesus!). I was unaware that our Our Lord Himself had given her a similar remedy in the words: 'Benedetto sio Dio e Maria!' (Blessed be God and Mary!) And the docile child, in order to obey both, used to repeat the double exclamation: 'Viva Gesu! Benedetto sio Dio e Maria!' The good spirits always repeated her words, whereas the malignant ones either did not reply, or else pronounced only a few words, such as 'Viva' or 'Benedetto', without adding any name. By this means Gemma recognized them and scorned them accordingly."*

Padre Pio was also one of the saints tormented by the devil in various forms. He was one of the victim souls who suffered with Christ for the salvation of souls. He spent up to 16 to 18 hours daily listening to confessions. One of Padre's close companions, Father Joseph Martin, O.F.M. Cap., tells the story of Padre Pio beaten so badly by the devil, causing him to fall on the floor of his cell, cutting his head. The following morning, Father Martin went to his cell asking what had happened. Padre Pio related to him that he was beaten by the devil. Blood stains were found on his pillow. The pillow is currently kept in his cell at Our Lady of Grace Friary. Padre Pio stated the Virgin Mary had placed the pillow under his bleeding head while consoling him.

In 1906, Padre Pio had one of his first contacts with the devil. One summer night, Padre Pio had returned to the convent of Saint Elia of Pianisi, and had difficulty sleeping because of the summer heat. Upon hearing footsteps from a nearby room he thought, "Apparently, Father Anastasio couldn't sleep either." He attempted calling the Father from the window, but was unable to speak. Padre Pio saw a monstrous dog on a ledge of a nearby window. With terror in his voice, he said, "I saw the big dog enter through the window and there was smoke coming from his mouth. I fell on the bed and I heard a voice from the dog that said, 'him it is, it is him.' While I was still on the bed, the animal jumped to the ledge of the window, then to the window, then disappeared."

In a letter to his personal director, Padre Pio describes being beaten by demons: "The ogre (devil) won't admit defeat. He has appeared in almost every form. For the past few days he has paid me visits along with some of his satellites armed with clubs and iron weapons and, what is worse, in their own form as devils. I cannot tell you how many times he has thrown me out of bed, and dragged me around the room. But never mind! Jesus, our dear Mother, my little Angel, St. Joseph and our father St. Francis are almost always with me." (Letter to Padre Agostino, Jan. 18, 1912)

Padre Pio was tormented by the devil continuously. Demons would appear to him in the form of a naked girl dancing, his guardian angel, his spiritual director, the Virgin Mary, an ugly black cat, or as a prison guard who would whip him. He would be beaten severely until he was bleeding, tormented with deafening howls, or covered in spit.

On one occasion, the devil, while taking the form of his spiritual director, knocked on his door. He told Padre Pio he was there to inform him that God was not pleased with his practice of penance. Padre Pio then asked for him to say the name of Jesus, whereby the apparition laughed. When Padre attempted to touch his robe, he vanished leaving a strong smell of sulphur. On July 28, 1914, speaking of this event he related: "The Devil, as you know, is a great artificer of evil...he could deceive you by some diabolical illusion or apparition disguised as an angel of light ...This unhappy apostate even knows how to disguise himself as a Capuchin and to act the part quite well. I beg you to believe one who has undergone an experience of this nature."

Another great saint who was spiritually and physically tormented by the devil, was St. Jean-Marie-

Baptiste Vianney, also known as "The Cure D'Ars."
The Cure D'Ars was born on May 8, 1786, in Dardilly,
France. He was a humble priest full of faith, who lived
his life eating only boiled potatoes. He had the gift of
reading souls, and so many traveled from long distances
to receive his spiritual counsel in confession. He spent
41 years as a parish priest of Ars, France, and died on
August 4, 1859. He was canonized on May 31, 1925.
His body remains incorruptible, and can be viewed
encased in glass in Ars, France.

"That hell exists and that there are fallen angels condemned

to hell, is a dogma of the Catholic faith. The devil is a personal,

living being, not a figment of the imagination. True, his activity in

the world remains for the most part hidden; none the less, by

divine permission, at times the evil one comes out into the open."

(Trochu, Abbe Francis, "The Cure D'Ars St. Jean-Marie-Babtiste

Vianney," Tan Books and Publishers, 1977)

The Cure of D'ars was known to save many souls,
and was therefore a prime target of Satan. He spent
most of the day in the confessional and had very little
time to sleep. Many times upon lying on a straw

mattress, he would be tormented with mournful cries and banging noises. On one occasion, the frightened saint was thrown from his bed by the devil. He then made the sign of the cross and the devil left him in peace. During these episodes, the Cure D'Ars was wearied, but never discouraged. When asked by his confessor how he repelled the attacks by the demon, he stated: *"I turn to God; I make the sign of the cross; I address a few contemptuous words to the devil. I have noticed, moreover, that the tumult is greater and the assaults more numerous if, on the following day, some big sinner is due to come."*

The saint relates one encounter: *"...last night the devil came into my room whilst I was reciting my breviary. He was blowing hard, and it seemed to vomit on my floor, I know not what, but it looked like either corn or some other grain. I told him: 'I am going over there (to the Providence) to tell them of thy behavior, so that they may despise thee!' and he stopped at once."*(Trochu, Abbe Francis, "The Cure D'Ars St. Jean-Marie-Babtiste Vianney," Tan Books and Publishers, 1977)

An ordinary operation of the devil to most men and women is by tempting them. Extraordinary operations of the devil include infestation, external obsession, internal obsession, and possession. In rare cases, the demons reveal themselves by terrifying vexations, by causing loud noises, and moving objects. This is known as infestation. Infestation is one of the diabolical occurrences the Cure D'Ars suffered from.

Another rare diabolical operation, known as external obsession, is where the demon physically attacks and hurts the obsessed person. The saint was also a victim of external obsession, but only on rare occasions. Internal obsession is where a soul is influenced by the demons sentiments. The Cure D'Ars did not relate whether he suffered from this obsession. Lastly, possession is where the demon takes possession of the human body.

As predicted by so many saints and mystics, these type of demonic operations will occur during the three days of darkness. As we see with these saints, it's entirely feasible the demons will take different forms to either trick, terrify, or discourage us. The demon can take on almost any form whether it is a family member, an acquaintance, or any type of vicious animal.

It's good to remember, that during the darkness, we should be very attentive that any contact with an individual or animal that causes uneasiness is not from

God. A simple prayer and faith will help distinguish whether we are being tricked by a fallen angel. Just as the saints who were tormented by the devil, God may wish to strengthen our faith during this tribulation.

As indicated by the prophecies, the three days of darkness will be a time of spiritual cleansing where our faith and prayer will cause us to prevail. As in all things, some may experience more challenges during these times more than others. Faith in God will prevent fear. Padre Pio wisely informs us to "pray unceasingly."

VI

Weapons Against Evil

"When the prayer of the Church commands the infernal spirit to leave, let us never be without the Cross on us which is the invincible weapon which overthrows him and forces him to return to hell." (Marie Julie Jaheny)

Evil will dominate the earth during the three days of darkness. What weapons should we have available to combat the demons? The saints and mystics advise to pray unceasingly and have a crucifix, blessed candles, blessed objects, and holy water available. These weapons and others have proved effective by Christians throughout history to combat evil.

We are reminded to place a blessed cross above all the doors outside our home for protection, and to retain a crucifix in the house. The cross is a sign of the sacrifice of Christ for the sins of all mankind and therefore is repulsive to the evil one. The sacred image of the cross has been venerated as far back as early Christianity and was used to strengthen Christians during times of persecution.

In the catechism of the Catholic Church we read, "There ought not to be a single church, or altar, or cemetery, without a crucifix." The church holds such an honor for the crucifix, that no sacrament can be administered and no mass celebrated without it. It states: "Above all representations of the saints or of holy things, we venerate the cross of Our Redeemer…this sacred symbol ought to be found in every Christian household…"

A blessed crucifix is a powerful weapon against evil. If the crucifix is effectively used during an exorcism, than it would surely be an asset during the three days of darkness against the demons. A crucifix is a cross with the body of Jesus Christ affixed to it. It is a fitting symbol to remind us of Jesus' sacrifice for mankind, his crucifixion. Jesus overcame Satan by dying for us, and thus mankind is delivered from darkness and granted the Kingdom of Heaven. However, Satan has not been completely abolished and still wanders the world searching for souls. This war against the devil continues by Christ and the Holy Church now and until the end of times. St. Paul exhorts us: *"Put on the armor of God so that you may be able to stand firm against the tactics of the devil. For our struggle is not with flesh and blood but with the principalities, with the powers, with the world rulers of this present darkness, with the evil spirits in the heavens. Therefore, put on the armor of God, that you may be able to resist on the evil day and, having done everything, to hold your ground."* (Ephesians 6:11-13)

One shield against the devil is baptism. Rev. Paul Sullins, a sociologist at the Catholic University in Washington D.C., states that the Catholic Church has seen a decline in infant baptism, even as the Church has shown an increase in members within the past half century. He further states, that even though births have declined, the baptismal rate has declined even more.

More people are failing to see the significance of this all important sacrament, not only in the Catholic Church, but Christians of all denominations. Coupled with an increase in spiritualism, more children are susceptible to evil influence more than ever.

In the account of "The life of Jesus Christ," by Catherine Emmerich, she describes many exorcisms Jesus performed. She describes how numerous the possessed were, and how they were open to the devil's attack with their lack of faith, pagan rituals and sorcery. Catherine describes her vision of Jesus casting out the demons from the unfortunate possessed. She later could see a black vapor rising from the body. On one occasion she describes "…a whole cloud of vapors issued from their bodies in numberless forms of insects, toads, worms, and chiefly mole-crickets."

Catherine Emmerich states that after ridding them of the demons, Jesus urged them to be baptized, and called them to penance. After being cured, they listened to Jesus' instructions, and he explained to them why so many were possessed in these parts. She states Jesus told them, "it was because the inhabitants were so intent upon the things of this world and so given up to the indulgence of their passions." Without the sacrament of baptism they did not possess the necessary spiritual strength to combat evil.

Baptism cleanses us from original sin and confers the gift of sanctifying grace of the Holy Spirit. We become a child of God. Baptism gives us the strength to fight the evil one. During Pentecost, St. Peter urges: "Repent and be baptized, every one of you, in the name of Jesus Christ for the forgiveness of your sins; and you will receive the gift of the Holy Spirit." (Acts 2: 38)

In 1949, baptism was instrumental in the exorcism of a 14 year old boy, who's story led to the making of the popular 1974 movie, "The Exorcist," written by William Peter Blatty. The movie portrays a possessed girl played by Linda Blair. Unable to obtain the church's official records of the exorcism, Blatty produced a fictionalized version. The boy was born on June 1, 1935.

The exorcist accounts that the boy was 13 years old when his parents and aunt used an Ouija board. Most exorcists contend that the Ouija board is an open invitation to the devil. After this, strange phenomenon began following the boy and eventually his possession. At least twenty exorcisms were performed on the boy before he was successfully freed from the demons that possessed him. His lack of baptism, coupled with the use of the Ouija board, may have opened the door for the demon.

Every family should consider baptism as the highest priority when a child is born. I have heard so often families stating they wish to forego baptism until the child is old enough to make his own decision on what faith they choose to be baptized. The child needs baptism to grow spiritually, as it fills the child with the Holy Spirit, and gives the child the strength to combat evil. Why would one forego this necessity?

The Scriptures also indicate baptism is necessary for salvation. "Unless a man be born again of water and of the Holy Ghost, he cannot enter into the kingdom of heaven."(John 3:5) Therefore, baptism should be the number one priority for the salvation of our soul, and in preparation for any future chastisement for children and adults alike.

Baptism is performed by pouring Holy Water on the head of the person. This leads us to the next weapon against evil that should be available in every home. Holy Water is a sacramental in the Catholic Church, and possesses a special power against demons. The evil one cannot be present long where Holy Water is present.

Changes were made to the Order for blessing water of the Roman Rite during the Second Vatican Council. The intention of the Second Vatican Council was a revision of the Order, but the changes were so drastic they completely transformed the Old Rite. The 1952 Rite, prior to the revisions, began with exorcising (banishing evil spirits) the salt, separately exorcising and blessing the water, and then mixing the salt with the water with a final blessing. The Rite's origin can be traced to Liturgical Books and Sacred Tradition.

In the current Order, the prayer used invokes a blessing on the people who use it in faith and allows for the blessing to be performed by a bishop, priest, or deacon. There are three prayers of blessings the celebrant may choose. One Novus Ordo blessing for Holy Water outside the mass is the following:

Blessed are you, Lord, Almighty God, who

deigned to bless us in Christ, the living water of

our salvation, and to reform us interiorly, grant

that we who are fortified by the sprinkling of or

use of this water, the youth of the spirit being

renewed by the power of the Holy Spirit, may

walk always in newness of life.

There is no exorcised salt added to the water, nor is the water exorcised. In contrast, the Roman Rite prayers exorcising the salt, explicitly call out for the casting out of demons. It includes praying for those who use it to be healthy, as well as a medicine for body and soul.

The prayers exorcising the salt and water from the previous Roman Rite are exceptionally beautiful. They are included here, so there's an understanding of the elements of the prayer, and how the blessed salt and water can be used as a protection against the devil:

> *God's creature, salt, I cast out the demon from*
>
> *you by the living God, by the true God, by the holy*
>
> *God, by God who ordered you to be thrown into*
>
> *the water spring by Eliseus to heal it of its*
>
> *barrenness. May you be a purified salt, a means of*
>
> *health for those who believe, a medicine for body*

and soul for all who make use of you. May all evil fancies of the foul fiend his malice and cunning, be driven afar from the place where you are sprinkled. And let every unclean spirit be repulsed by Him who is coming to judge both the living and the dead and the world by fire.

Almighty everlasting God, we humbly appeal to your mercy and goodness to graciously bless this creature, salt, which you have given for mankind's use. May all who use it find in it a remedy for body and mind. And may everything that it touches or sprinkles be freed from uncleanness and any influence of the evil spirit; through Christ our Lord.

Exorcism of the water:

God's creature, water, I cast out the demon from

you in the name of God the Father Almighty, in

the name of Jesus Christ, His Son, Our Lord,

and in the power of the Holy Spirit. May you be

purified water, empowered to drive afar all power

of the enemy, in fact, to root out and banish the

enemy himself, along with his fallen angels. We

ask this through the power of our Lord Jesus

Christ, who is coming to judge both the living and

the dead and the world by fire

O God, who for man's welfare established the

most wonderful mysteries in the substance of water,

hearken to our prayer, and pour forth your

blessing on this element now being prepared with

various purifying rites. May this creature of yours,

when used in your mysteries and endowed with

your grace, serve to cast out demons and to banish

disease. May everything that this water sprinkles

in the homes and gatherings of the faithful be

delivered from all that is unclean and hurtful; let

no breath of contagion hover there, no taint of

corruption; let all the wiles of the lurking enemy

come to nothing. By the sprinkling of this water

may everything opposed to the safety and peace of

the occupants of these homes be banished, so that

in calling on your holy name they may know the

well being they desire, and be protected from every

peril; through Christ our Lord.

In the form of a cross, the priest then pours the salt into the water and says:

May this salt and water be mixed together, in the

name of the Father, and of the Son, and of the

Holy Spirit. God, source of irresistible might and king of an invincible realm, the ever glorious conqueror, who restrain the force of the adversary, silencing the uproar of his rage, and valiantly subduing his wickedness, in awe and humility we beg you, Lord, to regard with favor this creature thing of salt and water, to let the light of your kindness shine upon it, and to hallow it with the dew of your mercy; so that wherever it is sprinkled and your holy name is invoked, every assault of the unclean spirit may be baffled, and all dread of the serpent's venom be cast out. To us who entreat your mercy grant that the Holy Spirit may be with us wherever we may be, through Christ our Lord.

Should one be concerned if the New Rite of blessing water is less efficacious than the Old Rite? Blessings are conferred on those who use the New Rite

Holy Water in faith. However, the Holy Water by the Old Rite is exorcised and its intention is to drive away evil influence. The Old Rite invokes the presence of the Holy Spirit wherever it is sprinkled. With this in mind, exorcised salt and exorcised "blessed" water, should be in every home to combat the evil influences now, and any future tribulations.

One of the least considered, but perhaps one of the strongest weapons against demonic influences, is confession. Many Catholics go to mass regularly, but rarely go to confession. There is some inherent fear of confessing your sins to a priest.

Hearing a priest say "Your sins are forgiven," lifts the burden of guilt. If this sacrament was used more regularly, fewer psychiatrists would be needed. The Catechism of the Catholic Church teaches by "worthily receiving this sacrament the guilt of sin is remitted, the Holy Spirit returns to the repentant sinner and imparts sanctifying grace, and through the Holy Spirit we obtain great peace of mind and the strength necessary to overcome sin." But how can confession prepare us for the three days of darkness or any future tribulations?

A prominent exorcist in Rome, Father Gabriele Amorth, describes in his book, "An Exorcist Tells His Story," his battle with diabolical possession, oppression, obsession, and infestation. His astonishing account of exorcisms exposes how alive and real demonic influences are today. As prophesied by the saints and mystics, the demons will be released from hell during the three days of darkness. These demons may manifest in several forms.

Father Amorth's confrontation with the evil one serves as an example of defending ourselves from these evil influences. He describes the means of safeguarding ourselves are in "prayer, the sacraments, almsgiving, leading a Christian life, pardoning offenses, and soliciting the aid of our Lord, Mary, the saints, and the angels." A profound statement of Father Amorth, "confession is stronger than an exorcist," expresses how confession is of the utmost importance. When we examine this statement, then it becomes clear, after confession we are filled with the Holy Spirit and given sanctifying grace. The evil one can no longer be present where the Holy Spirit abides. (There are exceptions of demonic obsession that God has allowed for saints like Padre Pio in order to fulfill his will.)

In the Old Testament, God commanded Moses that a lamp be filled with the purest Oil of Olives and should always be burning in the Tabernacle. (Exodus 40: 25) Historians have found that many ancient civilizations were using different forms of wicked candles made with wax from insects, plants, tree nuts, or boiling the fruit of the cinnamon tree. Candles were known to have been used in religious ceremonies as in 165 B.C., where candles were used during the Jewish ceremony, Hanukkah, the Festival of Lights.

It has been predicted that no man made lighting will work during these days of darkness:

"The candles of blessed wax alone will give light during this horrible darkness. One candle alone will be enough for the duration of this night of hell." (Marie Julie Jahenny)

"It will be impossible to use any man-made lighting during this darkness, except blessed candles." (Blessed Anna Maria Taigi)

"Light a blessed candle, which will suffice for many days."
(Padre Pio)

Beeswax candles, the purest form of wax, are required by the Catholic Church to be used during the Mass and other liturgical ceremonies. (luminaria cerea.—Missale Rom., De Defectibus, X, 1; Cong. Sac. Rites, September 4, 1875.) The pure wax is made by honey bees and extracted from the bee hive. This pure wax, made by virgin bees, is symbolic of Jesus' pure, unstained nature, born of the Virgin Mary. The candle wick is symbolic of Christ' soul, and the flame represents his divinity. The beeswax candle burns very clean without producing a smoky flame.

It is suggested to have 100% beeswax candles. These candles will need to be blessed and used with faith. Only one will be sufficient to last the three days. The blessed candles will not light for the unbelievers and scoffers. We must continually pray and be prepared.

The saints also recommended having blessed objects such as St. Benedict's medal, the rosary, and the scapular. No home should be without these blessed items to combat the evil one.

VII

Prayer During the Three Days

How do we pray during the three days of darkness? In the New Testament Jesus taught us how to pray by providing us with "The Our Father" prayer. By providing us with this prayer, He was showing us there are ways to pray that are preferred by Our Lord. He provided us with examples of holiness through his Mother, the Patriarchs, and the Saints. Through their example we can learn how to pray in a way that pleases the Lord.

The Catholic catechism teaches us that "prayer is the elevation of the heart to God." When we pray we should forget all things, and think only of God. In our prayers we should include praise, our petitions, and thanksgiving.

There are ways to pray to obtain a quicker response. When we pray we should include fasting and charity. As in Acts 10, Cornelius prayed constantly and gave alms generously, and an angel appeared to him informing him his prayers were heard.

Venerable Mary of Agreda, 1602-1665, was a 17th century Spanish nun, who had revelations of the life of the Blessed Virgin Mary. The inspirational book, "The Mystical City of God," translated from the original Spanish, by Fiscar Marison (Rev. George Blatter), describes in detail the Virgin Mary's life from her birth to her death. Throughout the book, she describes Holy Mary in prayer prostrate before the Lord.

Mary of Agreda describes the Virgin Mary as an infant in prayer: "The heavenly Child loving prostrate before the throne, rendered most acceptable and human thanks to the eternal Being."(P.93) Upon the Virgin's presentation in the temple, she describes Her again in prayer: "The Princess of heaven prostrated Herself on the pavement, and, remembering that is was Holy ground and part of the temple, She kissed it. In humble adoration She gave thanks to the Lord for this new benefit, and She thanked even the earth for supporting Her and allowing Her to stand in this Holy place…"(Pg. 109)

In her revelation of the Incarnation, Mary of Agreda, relates that the Almighty God prepared the Virgin Mary for nine days preceding this mystery with numerous gifts and graces. She describes Holy Mary at the beginning of this blessed novena, praying at midnight, prostrate in the presence of the Most High. Another example is during the birth of Christ; "She prostrated Herself before the throne of his Divinity and gave Him glory, magnificence, thanks and praise for Herself and for all creatures…" (Pg. 307)

From these examples of the Blessed Virgin Mary in prayer, we learn prayer to the Almighty is most befitting by prostrating ourselves in humble adoration, and testifying our worthlessness before God. We also learn from the Blessed Virgin, that prayer should include thanks and praise.

Fervent prayer with outstretched arms is also a form of praying that beseeches a quicker response. In this way, we pray in the manner Jesus was crucified. Moses prayed with his hands raised up during the battle between the Israelites and the Amalekites. (Exodus 17:11-13) As long as Moses kept his hands outstretched, Israel prevailed. When he lowered his hands, Amalek prevailed. Moses also told Pharaoh, that as soon as he left the city, he would extend his hands to the Lord, and the thunder and hail would cease, so that Pharaoh may know the earth belongs to the Lord. (Exodus 9:29) Many saints also prayed in this manner. When prayer is devout and sincere, our hands are lifted up and our arms our outstretched.

The "Nine Ways of Prayer," of Saint Dominic is a revered document written by an anonymous author sometime during 1260 and 1288. The document was most likely written by those who knew him personally. St. Dominic knew that bodily prayer could lift the soul to God. The various forms of praying include kneeling, prostrating, arms outstretched, and bowing. He was known to lay prostrate on the ground, face down, pleading with the Lord for forgiveness. Saint Dominic would retreat to a quiet place to read the Psalms and meditate. Even as he walked, he would pray.

The highest form of worship is the Liturgy. Innumerable graces are bestowed upon us when we attend Mass. Although, we will not be able to attend Mass during the three days of darkness, what better way to prepare for any coming tribulations by attending

Mass and sharing in the Sacrifice of Jesus Christ. In the sacrifice of the Mass, God gives abundantly more graces than any other source. When we participate in Mass, and receive communion, we are given the necessary strength and graces to combat evil. St. Francis of Sales says: *"prayers offered in union with the divine Victim have an inexpressible power; favors can be obtained at the time of Mass which can be obtained at no other."*

"Man's response to the God who is good to him is love, and loving God means worshipping him." Pope Benedict XVI, "The Spirit of the Liturgy" Ignatius Press, 2000.

Marie Julie Jahenny provided these prayers to be said to the Holy Cross during these disasters: *"I hail you, I adore you, I embrace you, oh adorable Cross of my Saviour. Protect us, keep us, save us. Jesus loved you so much, by His example I love you. By your holy image calm my fears, I only feel peace and confidence. Oh Jesus, conqueror of death, save us."*

"With all prayer and supplication, pray at every opportunity in the Spirit. To that end, be watchful with all perseverance and supplication for all the holy ones..." Ephesians 6: 18

VIII

Summary

Signs and warnings will precede this crisis; evil growing continuously, unprecedented earthquakes, devastating thunder and lightning, epidemics with no cure, famine, and tidal waves. These disasters will be so unprecedented that there will be no question that they are a sign of God's impending justice.

Marie Julie Jahenny prophesies it will occur on a Thursday, Friday, and Saturday, the days of the Holy Sacrament. We're also reminded no electricity will be available and only the blessed candles will light. This chastisement will be world wide.

To recap the prophecy of Blessed Anna Maria Taigi, we are reminded to cover all the windows and doors and not look out: "Nothing will be visible and the air will be laden with pestilence, which will claim principally but not exclusively the enemies of religion…He who out of curiosity opens his window to look out or leave his house will fall dead on the spot."

Padre Pio issues the same warning not to look out and urges us to pray continually: *"On the day, as soon as complete darkness has set in, no one shall leave the house or look from out of the window…In the days of darkness, My elect shall not sleep, as did the disciples in the garden of olives. They shall pray incessantly, and they shall not be disappointed in Me. I shall gather My elect. Hell will believe itself to be in possession of the entire earth, but I shall reclaim it."*

The message is the same: stay indoors, cover the windows, and do not look out. Continuously pray and be confident in the Lord's mercy.

Sister Faustina made many predictions and provided us with the Hour of Mercy prayers and novena. Jesus, and the Virgin Mary, told Sister Faustina she will prepare the world for the final coming. It was predicted these prayers would be said during the end times. Again, our perception of time is different from God's, and the end times could last years, to hundreds of years. However, the message of God's mercy should be taken into consideration during these troubled times and in preparation of coming tribulations.

Sister Faustina relates Jesus' words:

You will prepare the world for My final coming. (Diary 429)

Speak to the world about My mercy ... It is a sign for the end times. After it will come the Day of Justice. While there is still time, let them have recourse to the fountain of My mercy. (Diary 848)

Tell souls about this great mercy of Mine, because the awful day, the day of My justice, is near. (Diary 965).

I am prolonging the time of mercy for the sake of sinners. But woe to them if they do not recognize this time of My visitation. (Diary 1160)

Before the Day of Justice, I am sending the Day of Mercy. (Diary 1588)

He who refuses to pass through the door of My mercy must pass through the door of My justice. (Diary 1146).

Holy Mary's Words to Saint Faustina:

> *You have to speak to the world about His great mercy and prepare the world for the Second Coming of Him who will come, not as a merciful Savior, but as a just Judge. Oh how terrible is that day! Determined is the day of justice, the day of divine wrath. The angels tremble before it. Speak to souls about this great mercy while it is still the time for granting mercy.* (Diary 635).

Pope Francis declared a Holy Year of Mercy starting December 8, 2015, through November 20, 2016. He urged us to remember "God forgives always," and to participate in the sacraments, especially confession. Only twenty-six Jubilees have been celebrated since it began over seven hundred years ago. Only three have been "extraordinary," including this one recently declared by Pope Francis. This event seemingly strengthens the possibility of the fulfillment of the prophecy of the three days of darkness. Sister Faustina related Jesus' words: "Before the Day of Justice, I am sending the Day of Mercy." Could this refer to the year of Mercy? Is the "Day" of Justice after this year of Mercy? Could prayer and confession appease God's justice and delay this chastisement? Is **guilt** the driving force of this prophecy? *"…The stars of the heavens and their constellations will send forth no light; The sun will be dark at its rising, and the moon will not give its light. Thus I will punish the world for its evil and the wicked for their* **guilt**.*"*(Isaiah 13: 9-11)

We must spiritually prepare for these days of darkness, and remain trustful in the Lord's mercy. These predictions are not meant to scare us, but prepare us, and warn us to be ready. This journey of life God has given us is short compared to the future eternity that awaits us. Why waste this precious gift of life. Continual prayer will help us to fully see what God's will is for us. We are living in dangerous and turbulent times. Divine Justice is imminent! Pray!

"In all ages men have been divinely instructed in matters expedient for the salvation of the elect...and in all ages there have been persons possessed of the spirit of prophesy, not for the purpose of announcing new doctrines, but to direct human actions." -St. Thomas Aquinas, Summa Theologica

Bibliography

Allen, Thomas B., "Possessed," New York, Doubleday, 1993.

Bessieres, Albert, S.J. "Wife, Mother and Mystic" (The Life of Blessed Anna Maria Taigi) Originally published by Sans and Co. London, England, 1952.

Bullinger, E.W. "Number in Scripture, Its Supernatural Design and Spiritual Significance." Fourth Edition, Revised, London, Eyre & Spottiswoode, (Bible Warehouse) Ltd. 1921.

Dupont, Yves "Catholic Prophecy" Copyright Tan Books and Publishers Inc. 1970, 1973.

Esper, Joseph M. Rev., "After the Darkness", Queenship Publishing, 1997.

Galgani, Saing Gemma. "The Diary of Saint Gemma Galgani." Catholic Way Publishing. 2013.

Germanus C.P., Venerable Father and A.M. O'Sullivan. "The Life of St. Gemma Galgani." Tan Books. Revised Edition 2004.

Hebert, Albert J SM. "The Three Days' Darkness." Copyright 1986.

Kowalska, Sister M. Faustina. "Divine Mercy in My Soul." Marian Press. First Published 1987. Second Edition with revisions (6th printing): 1990.

Mary of Agreda, Venerable. "The Mystical City of God." Translated by Fiscar Marison. Tan Books and Publishers, Inc. 1978.

Ruffin, C. Bernard. "Padre Pio: The True Story." Our Sunday Visitor Publishing Division. Copyright 1991.

Schmoger, Carl E. Very Reverend, Life of Anne Catherine Emmerich, (2 vols.) Tan Books, reprint 1976.

Schmoger, Carl E. Very Reverend, Life of Jesus Christ and Biblical Revelations. Tan Books, reprint 1979.

Spirago, Rev. Francis,"The Catechism Explained, An Exhaustive Explanation of the Catholic Religion," Tan Books, reprint, 1993.

Trochu, Abbe Francis. "The Cure D'Ars, St. Jean-Marie Baptiste Vianney." Tan Books and Publishers Inc. Originally published in 1927.

Tugwell, Simon OP.,"The Nine Ways of Prayer of Saint Dominic," Hardcover, Dominican Publications, 1978.

Van Slyke, Daniel G., December 23, 2003 "The Order for Blessing Water: Past and Present," Essay (February 8, 2015)

Scripture quotations taken from the Saint Joseph
Edition of The New American Bible, Revised Edition,
Catholic Book Publishing Corp. New Jersey, 2010

Other Sources:

Dallaire, Glenn. "Mystics of the Church" *The Battle For
Souls, the Mystic Saints Versus the Demons*, Accessed
January 4, 2015.
http://www.mysticsofthechurch.com/2013/12/the-
battle-for-souls-mystic-saints-vs.html

Dallaire, Glenn. "Saint Gemma Galgani" *Attacks by the
Devil*, Accessed January 4, 2015.
http://www.stgemmagalgani.com/2008/09/saint-
gemma-versus-devil.html

Fish Eaters. "The Nine Ways of Prayer of St. Dominic."
Accessed December 7, 2014.
http://www.fisheaters.com/stdominic9ways.html

Ford, Dana and Mohammed Tawfeeq. "Extremists
Destroy Jonah's Tomb, Officials Say." Last modified
July 25, 2014. Accessed October 19, 2014.
http://www.cnn.com/2014/07/24/world/iraq-
violence/

Gaultier, Bill. "Growing Through a Dark Night of the
Soul." Last modified August 6, 2008. Accessed
September 7, 2014.
http://www.soulshepherding.org/2008/08/growing-
through-a-dark-night-of-the-soul/

Grossman, Cathy Lynn. "Rite of Baptism Trickles Away" *USA Today*. Last modified April 12, 2006. Accessed January 25, 2015. http://usatoday30.usatoday.com/news/religion/2006-04-12-baptism-trend_x.htm

Infallible Catholic, *Padre Pio's Triumph Over the Devil*, May 4, 2012. Accessed January 4, 2015. http://infallible-catholic.blogspot.com/2012/05/padre-pios-triumph-over-devil.html

Lawton, Kim A., "Mary's Last Earthly Home?" Our Sunday Visitor Inc., December 8, 1996. Accessed August 31, 2015. https://www.ewtn.com/library/MARY/LASTHOME.HTM

Ludgate, Simon, "New Shocking Evidence Points to Pole Shift." April 26, 2015. Accessed August 23, 2015. http://yournewswire.com/new-shocking-evidence-points-to-pole-shift/

MacMahon, Reverand J.R., "Beatification and Canonisation." Accessed October 19, 2014. http://www.catholicpamphlets.net/pamphlets/BEATIFICATION%20AND%20CANONISATION.pdf

Mintz, Zoe, "Exorcisms are on the Rise: Priests Point to Growing Fascination with the Occult." November 20, 2014. Accessed November 23, 2014. http://www.ibtimes.com/exorcisms-are-rise-priests-point-growing-fascination-occult-1721561

Padre Pio Devotions. " A Short Biography." Accessed October 26, 2014. http://padrepiodevotions.org/a-short-biography/

Patterson, Richard D. "The Use of Three in the Bible." February 26, 2008. Accessed August 17, 2014. https://bible.org/seriespage/use-three-bible

San Martin, Ines. "In a Surprise Move, Pope Francis Declares a Holy Year of Mercy"Accessed December 11,2015. http://www.cruxnow.com/church/2015/03/13/in-surprise-move-pope-francis-declares-a-holy-year-of-mercy/

Schulte, A.J. "Altar in Liturgy" Accessed March 1, 2015. http://oce.catholic.com/index.php?title=Altar_%28in_Liturgy%29

Sisters of the Holy Redeemer. "Mother Alphonse Maria Eppinger" Accessed November 9, 2014. http://www.sistersholyredeemer.org/history.html

Smith, Stephen. "100 Bible Verses About Darkness." OpenBible.info, July 24, 2015. Accessed August 17, 2014. http://www.openbible.info/topics/darkness

Society of the Little Flower. "Saint Therese of Lisieux." Accessed September 7, 2014. http://www.littleflower.org/abouttherese/learn/

Weller, Philip T. S.T.D. Copyright 1964 Philip T. Weller,"The Roman Ritual." Accessed February 8, 2015

https://www.ewtn.com/library/PRAYER/ROMAN2.
TXT

Williams, Thomas D., Ph.D. October 28, 2014, "Pope
Blesses Work of Exorcists" Last Modified October 28,
2014. Accessed November 2, 2014.
http://www.breitbart.com/Big-
Peace/2014/10/28/Pope-Blesses-Work-of-Exorcists